# THE DARK SIDE OF ILLEGAL IMMIGRATION: CAUSE FOR NATIONAL CONCERN?

> Calling an illegal alien an undocumented immigrant is like calling a burglar an uninvited houseguest.

> —Arizona Representative Russell Pearce[2]

For nearly two decades, capital and the market for goods, services, and workers of many types have woven an ever more intricate web of global economic and social interdependence. No aspect of this interdependence seems to be more visible to the publics of advanced industrial societies than the movement of people. And no part of that movement is proving pricklier to manage effectively, or more difficult for publics to come to terms with, than illegal migration.[3]

Illegal immigration to the United States (U.S.) is a serious problem, probably more than most Americans realize. Unauthorized migration, especially unauthorized migration originating in Mexico, remains a "lightening rod" issue in the U.S., often galvanizing public opinion and attracting the attention of U.S. policymakers.[4] Advocates of illegal immigration characterize nearly all migrants as legitimate, implying the real costs and benefits imposed on the rest of the population are temporary and less important than other issues. Without fear of being labeled a "xenophobic" or "anti-immigrant", I propose there is a "dark side" to illegal immigration that impacts the U.S. at both the national and local levels of our society.

According to statistics provided by the Pew Hispanic Center, there are approximately 12 million illegal aliens living in the U.S. today[5] Who are these individuals and why are they pouring into the U.S. in record numbers? Will this growing trend of illegal immigration, certain to influence U.S. foreign policy in the twenty-first century, change the character of our nation's population? What is the impact of illegal immigration on the American working class and the economy? Is this current trend of increasing illegal immigration a result of failed policy or lack of enforcement? What impact will it have on the safety and security of American citizens? What measures need to be undertaken to stem the tide of illegal migration? This paper attempts to answer these questions.

## Undocumented Immigrants vs. "Illegal Aliens"

"Illegal alien" is the official term used in legislation and by the border patrol for a person who has entered the country illegally or is residing in the U.S. illegally after entering legally.[6] The terms "undocumented worker" or "unauthorized immigrant" are often used by supporters to account for all undocumented individuals, including children and those who do not work, arguing that it is offensive to describe any human as "illegal", whether or not their behavior is illegal. The term "illegal" has the tendency to provoke fear and loathing, as it is intended to do. Immigration law violators are not immigrants in the true sense of the word. They are, as indicated in federal law, "aliens" who are in the U.S. in violation of the law.

There is a profound difference between individuals who legally apply for admission and fulfill all the requirements for admission (immigrants), and those who decide to enter the U.S. by crossing the borders without being inspected by an immigration officer at a Port of Entry (POE), with or without a valid passport and visa, or intentionally overstay their visa in violation of the law. Labeling such violators as "intending immigrants" only confuses the issue and juxtaposing these two categories is specious logic.[7] For consistency, I will use the term "illegal alien" throughout this paper to describe individuals who enter or are present in the U.S. without authorization of the federal government irrespective of their mode of entry. Although the experience of the documented, as a growing phenomenon, deserves attention in its own right, illegal immigration as a social and political issue in the U.S. is as much about the way immigration is structured, conceived, and legislated as it is about the illegal aliens themselves.[8]

## History of U.S. Immigration

America is a "nation of immigrants" and immigration has played an important role in American history. It is a point of pride. From across the world, immigrants have brought their hopes and dreams to America's shores in search of freedom – the freedom to strive, to achieve, and above all to be judged on their merits, not the color of their skin, their religion, or their national origin.[9] However, much of the issue today with illegal aliens stems from decades of minimal enforcement of immigration policies and preferential treatment to certain groups.

For the first fifty years of U.S. history, from 1790 to the early 1840s, immigration to the U.S. was quite modest. It was in the 1840s that a trickle turned into a stream, with triple the number of immigrants of the preceding decade.[10] As a result, America was created by settlers who were overwhelmingly white, British, and Protestant. Their values, institutions, and culture provided the foundation for and shaped the development of the U.S. in the following centuries. They initially defined America in terms of race, ethnicity, culture and religion.[11] By contrast, the second wave of immigration, which began in the mid 1800s and lasted until the immigration restriction laws of the 1920s, was a more diverse and controversial phenomenon bringing more Catholics and Jews, more Southern Europeans and non-English speakers from Germany, Ireland and Scandinavia.[12]

With World War II and the assimilation of large numbers of Southern and Eastern European immigrants and their offspring into U.S. society, ethnicity virtually disappeared as a defining component of national identity. So did race, following the achievements of the civil rights movement and the Immigration and Nationality Act (INA) of 1965.[13]

Historically, millions of immigrants were attracted to the U.S. because of this culture and their ability to assimilate. This latest wave, however, after 1965 has fueled a new diversity from Latin America, primarily from Mexico. Americans now see and endorse their country as multiethnic and multiracial. As a result, American identity is now defined in terms of culture and creed.[14]

## Contemporary Immigration Laws

The INA of 1965 overhauled the country's immigration laws in major ways and serves as the basis of immigration law enforcement today. It replaced the national origins system of 1952 that gave preferential treatment to Eastern Hemisphere immigrants with a system designed to give an equal chance to people of all nations to immigrate to the U.S.[15] By that time, increased immigration from countries of the Western Hemisphere, particularly Mexico and Latin America, began to raise concerns.

The Immigration Reform and Control Act (IRCA) of 1986 was created with the intention to reduce illegal immigration to the U.S., which was perceived as an economic problem for the U.S. economy. It included amnesty for 3.1 million illegal aliens (90% from Mexico) and a glide path to citizenship, increased Border Patrol activities, employer sanctions aimed at removing the lure of employment, and a special exemption for aliens employed in agricultural work.[16]

The INA of 1990 increased the number of legal immigrants allowed into the U.S., more than doubled the number of visas available to persons qualified for employment-based immigration, and provided exceptions to the English testing process required for naturalization.[17]

The Illegal Immigration Reform and Immigrant Responsibility Act (IIRIRA) of 1996 strengthened border patrols by adding thousands more Border Patrol and Department of Interior Enforcement Agents, restricted judicial authority to review deportation cases, set greater penalties for the smuggling of immigrants and authorized voting by non-citizens.[18] Also, in part as a response to the 1993 World Trade Center bombing, Congress strengthened the anti-terrorism provisions in the INA and IIRIRA.

None-the-less, immigration boomed to a 57.4% increase in foreign-born population from 1990 to 2000. The public started to focus on existing immigration laws and immigration outside the law, especially the 7.5+ million illegal alien workers with 12+ million household members already inside the U.S. and another 700,000 to perhaps more than 850,000 predicted for each coming year.[19] At issue was whether the immigration laws and enforcement system were working, as the public wanted them to work.

In the most recent attempt to solve the issue of immigration (both legal and illegal), on 1 March 2003, the INS enforcement branch, which includes border enforcement and the investigations unit (interior enforcement), became part of the Department of Homeland Security (DHS) – Bureau of Immigration and Customs Enforcement (BICE). Under current law, two other departments along with DHS – the Department of State (DOS) and the Department of Justice (DOJ) play a key role in administering the law and policies on the admission of aliens. The DHS is focused on preventing terrorists from entering the U.S., its Citizenship and Immigration Services (USCIS) is charged with approving immigration petitions and its Bureau of Customs and Border Protection (CBP) is tasked with inspecting all people who enter the U.S. The DOS's Bureau of Consular Affairs is the agency responsible for issuing visas and DOJ's Executive Office for Immigration Review (EOIR) has a significant policy role through its adjudicatory decisions on specific immigration cases.[20]

The Push North: Mexico and Latin America

Migration from south of the border did not just happen; it was encouraged and supported by the U.S. government. In the latter half of the nineteenth century, the significant immigration of Mexicans to the U.S. was initiated by individual U.S. states to attract "cheaper" and more "pliable" labor.[21] The most attractive feature of Mexican labor was its temporariness, or so it was thought. Due to the proximity of Mexico to the U.S., many in the U.S. promoted immigration policies that allowed Mexicans to remain in the U.S. only as long as their labor was needed. Once their work was completed, they could return to Mexico. Although this cultivated animosity between Mexicans and other laborers, U.S. employers reasoned that Mexican workers were merely doing work unsuitable for "real" Americans.[22]

Around 1910, after the Mexican revolution, Mexicans began to migrate to the U.S. in record numbers attracted by a strong demand for labor, especially in the Southwest. However, in the 1930's, thousands were deported as U.S. unemployment rose sharply. Soon thereafter, spurred on by the shortage of agricultural labor during World War II, the first major Mexican migration regime took place after Congress signed the 1942 Bracero Accord. This measure permitted Mexicans to migrate temporarily for agricultural employment in the U.S. and began a twenty-two year period that legally sanctioned Mexican workers to meet the labor demands of U.S. farmers. Although both governments, Mexico and the U.S. shared responsibility for management of Bracero, it was the Mexican government that pressured the U.S. to enforce its southern border and adopted its own strategies to discourage illegal immigration.[23]

The Bracero Accord was officially terminated in 1964. However, illegal aliens were recruited in large numbers well after the Bracero program.[24] For almost ten years, Mexico unsuccessfully pressured the U.S. to implement a new temporary worker program; the U.S. refused. Without a temporary worker program in place, the Mexican government operated (until the mid-1980s) with a "no-policy" policy. What we today understand to be a crisis of illegal aliens from Mexico has its official roots in the demise of the Bracero program. Employers had become accustomed to cheap Mexican labor and were willing to ignore the fact that many of their employees were not legally residing in the U.S. with proper immigration documents. Although the Bracero Accord sparked the migration of many Mexicans, who later obtained legal status and sponsored eligible family members, changes in U.S. immigration policy after 1965 curtailed this opportunity. As a result, most Mexicans were unable to obtain legal status and illegal immigration surged.[25] This contributed to a rapid growth of Mexican illegal aliens in the U.S. over the past 35 years; a trend that shows no signs of slowing down.

About 80 to 85 percent of the immigration from Mexico and Central America in recent years has been illegal.[26] Apprehensions by the U.S. Border Patrol rose from 1.6 million in 1960s to 8.3 million in the 1970s, 11.9 million in the 1980s, and 14.7 million in the 1990s.[27] Today, illegal immigration of Mexicans and other Latin Americans through the porous 1700 miles of border dividing Mexico and the U.S. remains a serious problem. The statistics highlighted above indicate that the illegal alien problem is both a border and an interior enforcement problem though the INS has never placed much emphasis on interior enforcement.[28] The continuation of illegal immigration despite legislative, administrative, and enforcement initiatives over the last three decades represents a clear failure of national sovereignty and economic security objectives of U.S. immigration policy.[29] It is claimed that what the U.S. took from Mexico by conquest in 1848 will be repatriated to Mexico via the seeping wave of illegal immigrants, perhaps by the century's end.[30]

The Drivers Behind Illegal Immigration

Many illegal aliens seek higher wages and better standards of living than available to them in their country of origin. During the 1980s, it was estimated that some 7 million Mexicans lived and worked illegally in the U.S. - roughly 10 percent of Mexico's total population.[31] Poverty, overpopulation, Mexico's law extractive and distributive capabilities, and governmental corruption are the root causes of the moving north of millions of economic refugees.[32] As a student living in Mexico, I have seen first hand the country's misdistribution of income between the very few rich and the multitudes of the very poor.

Other illegal aliens migrate to the U.S. to escape civil war and seek political asylum. Although Salvadorans and Nicaraguans had been migrating to the U.S. for decades in smaller numbers when immigration laws were far more relaxed, they remained relatively invisible, "passing," or often being mistaken, for Mexicans. Most of these early arrivals easily obtained documents including green cards and U.S. citizenship. In 1979, the situation changed dramatically. Many left their countries at a moment's notice or, in any case, under extreme situations of danger. Because of their greater number and stiffened U.S. immigration policies, they have been unsuccessful at obtaining legal status. This has affected the jobs they have been able to find as well as their prospects for mobility, the reunification of families, and their children's (many of whom are U.S. citizens) future success. Though immigrants because of their situation, they are still classified as illegal aliens because of their lack of legal status.[33]

Ironically, because of its reputation as a major source of undocumented aliens to the U.S. and because of similar differences in wages and poverty between countries of origin, Mexico itself experiences this kind of immigration from Central America. Many undocumented Central American aliens in Mexico ultimately try to enter the U.S.[34] Unfortunately, Mexicans and South and Central Americans are not the only "illegals" crossing the Mexican border. Increasingly, global trafficking and human smuggling networks use that border as one option for delivering their clients from Europe, Asia, and the Middle East into the U.S. I will discuss this in more detail later in the paper.

Other immigrants seek to be reunited with families. Some choose to let the immigration system work for them; many do not. Even with children or spouses who are legal immigrants or U.S. citizens, individuals who enter this country to reunite their families without proper documentation are here illegally and have an impact on the U.S. It is obvious that between Mexico and the U.S one sees a spectrum of issues and problems involving this unprecedented clandestine migration in the Western Hemisphere.[35] Even Mexico's National Population Council is predicting that large-scale Mexican migration to the U.S. will continue for decades.[36] What will be the long-term effects of this next great illegal migration to our nation?

Characteristics of the Illegal Aliens

In January 2000, the INS estimated there were 7 million illegal aliens in the U.S.[37] The Pew Hispanic Center estimated that number increased to 10.3 million in March 2004 (including 1.3 million children under the age of 18) with illegal Mexicans numbering 5.9 million (57%) of the total and about 75% of all illegal aliens are of Latin American origin from El Salvador, Nicaragua, Guatemala, Columbia, Honduras, Ecuador, Dominican Republic, and Brazil. Asia, at about 1.0 million, represents 9%. Europe and Canada account for 6% and Africa about 4%.[38] With a growth rate of half a million a year, the National Research Center (NRC) estimates that by the year 2050, two thirds of the total population growth (approximately 80 million) will be migrants.[39] An estimated 42 million of them will be illegal – about half of the overall projected growth in the immigrant population.

Historically, the illegal alien population was highly concentrated in the Southwest corridor of the U.S. Since the 1990s, however, the most rapid growth in the illegal alien population has taken place in new settlement areas where the foreign-born had previously been a relatively small presence. Today, almost two-thirds live in eight states: California (24%), Texas (14%), Florida (9%), New York (7%), Arizona (5%), Illinois (4%), New Jersey (5%), and North Carolina (3%). Another 32% (3.1 million) live in 17 new settlement states stretching from the northwest through the mountain states to the southeast. Illegal alien families contain 13.4 million persons, including the 8.8 illegal migrant adults and 1.6 million children (under 18), and 3 million children who are U.S. citizens by birth. Most of the adults are relatively young, and though most of them work they have relatively low levels of education, which translates into low income, high poverty levels, and lack of health insurance.[40] This dispersed low-educated population tremendously impacts the entire nation.

Cause for National Concern

Illegal immigration has been a longstanding issue in the U.S., creating immense controversy. The mainstream media, and advocates of illegal aliens, tend to report only on illegal aliens who have done what most legal immigrants do; work hard and succeed (though without proper documentation to be in the U.S.). What they rarely report on are any of the negative aspects of illegal immigration. As President Bush stated in his address to the nation on Immigration Reform in May of 2006, "Illegal immigration puts pressure on public schools and hospitals, it strains state and local budgets, and brings crime to our communities. These are real problems."

It is important to take a look at the "dark side" of illegal immigration, facts of which most Americans are likely unaware, but that profoundly affect our national security and show just how vulnerable we are.[41] Here is a broad summary on how illegal immigration affects America and why this issue is a cause for national concern:

- easy conduit for terrorists entering the U.S.;

7

- escalation in crime;
- 300,000 additional prisoners to support for years;
- increases Balkanization of U.S.;
- increases multiculturalism/segregation/divisivism instead of the American melting pot;
- increases desire for Aztlan (reclaiming southwest states for Mexico);
- increases number of traffic accidents;
- main contributor to surging U.S. population;
- increases impact on infrastructure, including education;
- destruction of fragile ecosystems in American southwest;
- main cause of emergency rooms and hospitals closing as well as service cutbacks;
- introduction of third world diseases;
- increases welfare rolls (about 40% of illegal aliens are on welfare); and
- cost to U.S. taxpayers is about $55,000 each, over and above their tax contributions.[42]

Threat to National Security

"Illegal immigration just may be the way that the next horrific attack on American soil is enabled. Both before and after the September 11 attacks, terrorists have and will continue to exploit the weaknesses of our lax immigration system by committing fraud and other violations."[43] However, since the September 11 attacks, the nation has recognized a need for tighter immigration enforcement and border controls. As a nation, Americans now understand that our immigration policies are too easily exploited by terrorists and that porous borders and lax immigration enforcement provide the capability for terrorists to enter the U.S. virtually undetected.

The 4 March 2004 congressional testimony of Jessica M. Vaughan, Senior Policy Analyst for the Center for Immigration Studies is very compelling and makes an excellent case on the connection between illegal aliens, lax immigration laws and terrorism:

> We know that the 9/11 attacks were made possible in part due to failures in our immigration system, specifically our temporary visitor program. The 9/11 terrorists obtained visas they were not entitled to, they successfully used altered documents, and they overstayed their visas. Over the years, many of the terrorists we have caught have some immigration violation on their record, and virtually every immigration benefits program we offer has been exploited by terrorists. These abuses will likely continue unless we design a system that can snuff out the abuse with better information, better technology, better legal and policy guidelines, and better training. This system can only be designed if the agency that processes our immigration benefits, the U.S. Citizenship and Immigration Services, is considered and treated as a full partner in national security and border security agendas and these gaps in our immigration system

will remain exploited until the system becomes designed to catch terrorists better and provide sufficient resources and the political will to enforce the law.[44]

Terrorists easily take advantage of the overwhelming number of applications and the ease with which the system can be manipulated due to its perpetual state of inadequate information technologies. The result is that fraud runs rampant in applications for immigration benefits, with estimates provided to the 9/11 Commission by a senior official at the U.S. Center for Immigration Studies (CIS) to be anywhere from 50 to 75 percent.[45] No matter what the terrorist organization or mission, it is clear from this study that terrorists will continue to try to come to the U.S. to carry out operations, and their instructions will continue to include immigration-related plans. Until we have a system designed to weed out terrorists, their plans on how to stay in the U.S. will likely succeed.[46]

America must also be concerned with the growing connection between Latin America and Hezbollah, a Lebanese umbrella organization of radical Islamic Shiites that has been designated by the U.S. as a terrorist organization. Recently, an organization calling itself Hezbollah America Latina (Hezbollah LA) took responsibility for a 23 October 2006 attack on the American embassy in Caracas, Venezuela. The group also threatened to explode a non-lethal device against an ally of the U.S. in one Latin American city several months earlier in an attempt to launch its propaganda campaign and show its solidarity with the Lebanese Hezbollah after the war in Lebanon.[47] According to its website, Hezbollah LA is active in El Salvador, Columbia, Venezuela, Argentina, Mexico, and Chile. On 6 December 2006, the Bush administration targeted several individuals in Argentina, Brazil and Paraguay for providing "financial and logistical support" to Hezbollah.[48]

Islamic values are already present in Latin American culture. Now, at a time when Latin America is searching for its own identity and the common people are clearly looking forward to a totally different spiritual change, Latin America is a fertile area for Islamic dawah.[49]

Lastly, there is the possibility that the Lebanese Hezbollah and al-Qaeda will recruit "converted" Latin American terrorists for their operational terrorist international activity; as they did in the past in the Middle East and Europe.[50] Adm. James Loy, a former Deputy Secretary at the DHS, has said that intelligence "strongly suggests" al Qaeda is eyeing the southern border (between the U.S. and Mexico) as a "path of least resistance" to strike inside the U.S.[51] As evidence to support his argument, in fiscal year 2004, the Border Patrol had 155,000 arrests of illegal aliens from countries "other than Mexico;" about 700 of them were from "special interest countries," including Afghanistan, Iraq, Yemen, and Saudi Arabia. This is almost a 200%

increase from the number of arrests in fiscal year 2002 of only 37,316. "It's a whole different type of (illegal) immigrant coming over the border," asserts Texas Senator John Cornyn.[52]

Though much of the recent focus has been on illegal immigrants of Middle Eastern descent as perpetrators of the 11 September terrorist attacks, on 28 August 2006, Judicial Watch, the public interest group that investigates and prosecutes government corruption, obtained records from the DHS through the Freedom of Information Act (FOIA). The records consist of annual intelligence summaries of "Mexican Government Incidents," compiled over a nine-year period between 1996 and 2005 that document 226 incursions by Mexican government personnel into the U.S. The intelligence summaries provide detailed maps of the incursions, along with descriptions of other documented "incidents" involving Mexican government personnel and Border Patrol agents. The records describe incidents involving shots fired on both sides of the border, unmarked helicopters invading U.S. airspace, drug smuggling, and confrontations between U.S. Border Patrol agents and armed members of the Mexican military.

Increased Criminal Activity within the U.S.

The question of what role illegal aliens play in U.S. crime is a highly disputed subject. However, there is an enormous number of Americans who have been harmed by the criminals who pass through the nation's open borders via human smuggling, drug trafficking, homicides, sexual assault and a variety of other crimes.

Despite passage of the National Anti-Smuggling Program, toughened U.S. border enforcement has prompted substantially more illegal aliens to hire smugglers to help them cross over from Mexico - and competition among sophisticated criminal networks for customers has spawned violence and sometimes death.[53] In the case of crossing the U.S. – Mexico border, this has ranged from self-smuggling, to local-level individual smuggling entrepreneurs (the traditional "coyotes"), to highly organized and sophisticated transnational smuggling networks (often specializing in the smuggling of non-Mexicans across the border – such as Chinese and Central Americans).[54]

There are linkages between alien smuggling (synonymous with human trafficking) and organized crime for the purpose of sexual or economic oppression and exploitation.[55] Poverty and lack of economic opportunity make women and children vulnerable to false promises of job opportunities in other countries. Many of those who accept these offers from what appear to be legitimate sources find themselves in situations where their documents are destroyed, their selves or their families threatened with harm, or they are bonded by a debt they have no chance of ever repaying.

10

Human trafficking is not limited to sexual exploitation.  It also includes persons who are trafficked into "forced" marriages or into bonded labor markets, such as sweatshops, agricultural plantations, or domestic service.[56]  The fight against human trafficking has become a major focus of the Regional Consultation Group on Migration, composed of Belize, Canada, Costa Rica, El Salvador, Guatemala, Honduras, Mexico, Nicaragua, Panama and the U.S. encouraging participating states to pass legislation to outlaw alien smuggling.[57]

Mexico and countries in Central America lie directly between the drug producing countries in South America and drug consumers in the U.S.  Geographically, these nations provide a natural conduit for illicit drug trafficking organizations, which threaten our national security and influence governments throughout the region.  According to the U.S. Drug Enforcement Agency (DEA) homepage, illegal aliens and migrant workers frequently smuggle heroin (and other drugs) across the U.S. - Mexico border for the major trafficking groups.  In November 2005, a ranking DEA official testified before a Congressional panel that Mexican traffickers supplied 77% of the cocaine, 53% of the methamphetamine and approximately 50% of the heroin that enters the U.S.[58]  The DEA states this region will remain the primary transit zone for U.S.-bound drugs produced in Central and South America for the foreseeable future.

In the last decade, Mexico has received illegal immigrants as the result of civil war in Central America, many of whom attempt to eventually cross the U.S. border illegally.  Some who have been successful at entering the U.S. illegally are members of the Mara Salvatrucha, also know as MS-13, a criminal organization whose members have terrorized various places in Mexico and Latin America, and in the U.S. have spread across 33 states.[59]  MS-13 is one of the most dangerous gangs in America according to the FBI website.  Gang crime is exploding nationally—rising 50 percent from 1999 to 2002—driven by the march of Hispanic immigration east and north across the country.[60]

Unfortunately, there are no federal statistics maintained on murders or any other crimes committed by illegal aliens.  There are, however, a number of groups that have produced estimates based on data collected from prisons, news reports and independent research.  According to 2006 statistics released by Representative Steve King, Republican-Iowa, twelve Americans are murdered every day by illegal aliens.[61]  If those numbers are correct, that equates to 4,380 Americans murdered annually by illegal aliens.  To put these statistics in perspective, illegal aliens murdered 21,900 Americans since 11 September 2001, more than those killed in the Global War on Terror during this same time period.  This number represents only a fraction of the blood spilled by American citizens as a result of an open border and unenforced immigration laws. King contends that daily, drunk illegal alien drivers kill thirteen Americans and that eight American children daily are victims of sexual abuse by illegal aliens.[62]

Additionally, based on a one-year-in-depth study that included serial rapes, serial murders, sexual homicides and child molestation committed by illegal aliens, Deborah Schurman-Kauflin of the Violent Crimes Institute of Atlanta, estimates there are about 240,000 illegal alien sex offenders in the U.S. who have an average of four victims each.[63] "This translates to 93 sex offenders and 12 serial sexual offenders coming across U.S. borders illegally per day," Schurman-Kauflin says. According to the study, the highest number of sex offenders come from Mexico. El Salvador was the original home to the next highest number. Other countries of origin included Brazil, China, Ecuador, Guatemala, Honduras, Jamaica, Nicaragua, Puerto Rico, Russia, and Vietnam.[64] What I found most startling was that, according to the study, 63% of these offenders had been deported on another offense prior to the sex crime and had, simply, returned to the U.S. to continue their criminal activities.

According to Edwin Rubenstien, president of ESR Research Economic Consultants, in 1980, federal and state correctional facilities held fewer than 9,000 criminal aliens. At the end of 2003, that number increased significantly and approximately 267,000 illegal aliens were incarcerated in all U.S. jails and prisons;[65] all supported by U.S. citizens' tax dollars. In April 2005, the Government Accountability Office (GAO) released a report on a study of 55,322 illegal aliens incarcerated in federal, state, and local facilities during 2003. The 55,322 illegal aliens studied represented a total of 459,614 arrests – some eight arrests per illegal alien. Their arrests represented a total of about 700,000 criminal offenses – approximately 13 offenses per illegal alien.[66] One can easily deduce that as the number of illegal aliens in the U.S. increases, so will the number of American victims

An analysis of the types of illegal alien removals from the U.S. completed by the INS reflects that criminal removals are far fewer than the non-criminal removals. This seems to reflect that little has changed in the overall priority of INS to concentrate on low-level visa abusers (non-criminal) rather than more serious offenders. The GAO concluded that INS failed to locate at least half of the deportable aliens in prison (other than INS custody) and this cost the U.S. almost $40 million in subsequent detention costs.[67]

Impact on the US Economy

Some economists have argued that whether the impact of illegal aliens on the U.S. economy has been good or bad depends on which section of the U.S. population you are concerned about the most. There is a continuing sensitivity to immigration impacts, especially illegal aliens' impact on wages and job opportunities for natives. A second concern is whether these effects are especially disadvantageous for certain groups. A third concern is about the relative usage of public services.[68] A fourth concern is the growing financial burden to both state and local governments.

Many U.S. employers rely on undocumented labor (illegal aliens) and many other American businesses are willing to hire cheap, compliant labor from abroad. Such businesses are seldom punished because our country lacks a viable system to verify new hires' work eligibility. Illegal aliens are especially popular with many employers because they can pay less than the legal minimum wage or have unsafe working conditions, secure in the knowledge that few unauthorized workers will report the abuse to the authorities.[69]

The NRC Study of 1997 concluded that, in areas with large immigrant communities, there are adverse effects for wages of certain types of native workers. The cost of labor has cheapened and this has benefited business owners, but had a detrimental effect on the American poor.[70] Most affected are those lacking a high school education, with whom recent immigrants (or illegal aliens) may have promoted wage and job competition. Those at the bottom of the economic ladder are disproportionately African-American, Hispanic, female and unskilled.[71]

Not all of this labor is low-wage, nor is all of it as vital to economic interests as may be argued by employers. Nevertheless, as a labor issue, undocumented immigration raises difficult questions about the structure of the American economy and how it continues to see low-wage labor and avoids extraneous labor costs such as health benefits, retirement packages, worker protection from injury in dangerous work, and worker protection from disability in debilitating jobs.[72] There is something fundamentally wrong with the American economic system in which employers cannot afford or choose not to provide a normal employment contract to its employees. The desperation with which workers from other countries (particularly Mexico and Latin America) will nevertheless accept such conditions is an equally damning indictment of the existing efforts to spread development and some measure of prosperity more broadly throughout the world.[73]

There are constant debates that illegal aliens are only doing the work that no American wants to do. According to George Borjas, a Harvard economist, "it is not that American natives do not want the jobs that immigrants do; it is that they do not want to the jobs at the wages immigrants are currently paid."[74]

Issues related to illegal immigration to the U.S. include research that such immigration has hidden medical consequences, such as the importation of diseases, which some sources describe as serious. Since aliens without proper legal status have no valid identification documents such as identity cards, they may have reduced or no access to public health systems, proper housing, education and banks. This lack of access results in the creation or expansion of an illegal underground economy to provide these services.[75] The unexpected appearance of many children (either illegal themselves or the offspring of illegal aliens) may challenge school systems, and use of hospital emergency rooms by those with no access to other kinds of health care may strain resources.[76]

A study conducted by the CIS in 2004 estimates that in 2002, households headed by illegal aliens used $10 billion more in government services than they paid in taxes, creating a fiscal burden on the federal budget. This figure is only for the federal government; costs at the state and local level are also likely to be significant.[77] The study also finds that if illegal aliens were given amnesty (as proposed by the President in 2006), the fiscal deficit at the federal level would grow to nearly $29 million.[78] The net deficit is caused by a low level of tax payments by immigrants, because they are disproportionately low skilled and thus earn low wages, and a higher rate of consumption of government services, both because of their relative poverty and their higher fertility rates.

The national interest dictates that priority must always be to prepare citizens and resident alien workers for jobs in the expanding employment sectors of the economy. Illegal immigrants can fill the jobs, but the social cost to the nation is a loss of opportunities to build a better society with all of the attendant social and human costs that will result.[79] The costs of illegal immigration in terms of government expenses for education, criminal justice, and emergency medical care are significant. The fact that states must bear the cost of federal failure turns illegal immigration, in effect, into one of the largest unfunded federal mandates.[80] As the size of the illegal alien population continues to increase, so will the loss.

A Shift in the Balance of Political Power

Politicians and religious groups have a vested interest in not enforcing interior immigration laws. Such groups stand to receive benefits from a larger alien population — one for votes, the other for potential converts. A little noticed effect is the way in which immigration impacts the distribution of seats in the U.S. House of Representatives. Apportionment is based on each state's total population — including illegal aliens and other non-citizens defined as legal immigrants, temporary visitors mainly foreign students and guest workers — relative to the rest of the country.

In 2000, the presence of illegal aliens in other states caused Indiana, Michigan, and Mississippi to each lose one seat in the House, while Montana failed to gain a seat it otherwise would have. In addition to these four states that lost a seat due to the presence of illegal aliens, Oklahoma, Pennsylvania, Wisconsin, Kentucky, and Utah each had one fewer seat than they otherwise would have. In the nine states that lost a seat due to the presence of non-citizens, only one in 50 residents is a non-citizen. In contrast, one in seven residents is a non-citizen in California, which picked up six of these seats and one in 10 residents is a non-citizen in New York, Texas, and Florida, the states that gained the other three seats.

None of the states that lost a seat due to non-citizens is declining in population. The population of the four states that lost seats due to illegal immigration increased 1.6 million in the 1990s, while the population of the five states that lost seats because of other non-citizens grew by two million. Apparently, immigrant-induced reapportionment is different from reapportionment caused when natives relocate to other states. Immigration takes away representation from states composed almost entirely of U.S. citizens and results in the creation of new districts in states with large numbers of non-citizens.[81]

Illegal immigration not only redistributes seats in the House, it has the same effect on presidential elections because the Electoral College is based on the size of congressional delegations. The political stakes for low-immigration states are enormous. The political costs to American citizens are clearly something to consider when debating immigration policy.[82]

A Lack of National Interest

Most Americans see the creed and culture as the crucial element of their national identity. Key elements of that culture include the English language; Christianity; religious commitment; English concepts of the rule of law, including the responsibility of rulers and the rights of individuals; and dissenting Protestant values of individualism, the work ethic, etc. Historically, millions of migrants were attracted to the U.S. because of this culture and the economic opportunities and political liberties it made possible.[83]

The extent and nature of this immigration differ fundamentally from those of previous immigration. Unlike past immigrant groups, Mexicans and Latinos have not assimilated into mainstream U.S. culture, forming instead their own political and linguistic enclaves – from Los Angels to Miami – and rejecting the values that built the American dream.[84] This lack of assimilation poses a potential threat to the country's cultural and political integrity and the persistent inflow of Hispanic immigrants threatens to divide the U.S. into two peoples, two cultures, and two languages.[85]

If the spread of Spanish as the U.S.'s second language continues, it could, in due course, have significant consequences in politics and government. In many states, those aspiring to political office might have to be fluent in both languages. Bilingual candidates for president and elected federal positions would have an advantage over English-only speakers. The ramifications are startling but have received little public attention or meaningful discussion. Just imagine, elementary and secondary school teachers will increasingly be expected to be bilingual. Government documents and forms could routinely be published in both languages. The use of both languages could be acceptable in congressional hearings and debates. In the end, Americans who speak only English will be disadvantaged.

## The Government's Proposed Way Ahead

President Bush's immigration reform package, stalled in Congress in 2006, proposes a radical immigration agenda that is designed to satisfy business' demands for an endless supply of low wage labor and create a legal path for foreign workers to come to our country via a new "Bracero-like" work program. It provides for increased border security from the use of technology to increase in personnel and outlines provision for catching and managing illegal detainees by eliminating the futile provision of "catch and release." These measures are all well intended, but without adequate and continuous resourcing and rigorous and continuous enforcement, they will be much like the immigration reform efforts of the past – simply on the books that no one bothers to adhere to.

Where the President falls short in his immigration reform is a suitable resolution for the nearly 12 million illegal immigrants currently living in the U.S. President's Bush current plan reads much like the amnesty program of 1965 whereby millions of illegal immigrants will be rewarded and provided an easy glide path to legality. With the change in congressional leadership (from Republican to Democratic), President Bush is hopeful that 2007 will be the year he finally succeeds in passing his guest worker and amnesty plan that has been consistently rejected by the American public and the majority of his own party.[86] The plan, though it will offer relief to farmers and others who claim they need unskilled labor, temporary legal status to the illegal worker, does little to provide a permanent solution addressing the 12 million illegal aliens currently living in the U.S. Additionally, amnesty has the potential to exacerbate the problem by encouraging more individuals to enter the country illegal.

## A Balanced Approach to an Age Old Problem

Illegal immigration is a cause for national concern and in order to solve the problem, a completely new approach is needed and it should be done in such a way that does not rob

America of more well meaning, law abiding immigrants. There are four primary reasons for the systemic failure of the immigration system. First, as I have shown, law and order measures alone are ineffective. Even with the National Guard and an almost militarized border, the U.S. has been less than successful in stemming illegal movement. Second, immigration systems bind the sending and receiving countries together, creating dynamics that feed and encourage ever more migration. Third, unless the U.S. buries itself in isolation, everything it does globally has economic, political and cultural consequences and an impact on immigration. Fourth, people fleeing circumstances they consider intolerable will enter the illegal migration quagmire and test the defenses in place regardless of the consequences.[87]

Controlling illegal immigration requires a balanced approach with a full range of enforcement improvements that go far beyond the border. These include many procedural reforms, beefed up investigation capacity, asylum reform, documents improvements, major improvements in detention and deportation procedures, limitations on judicial review, improved intelligence capacity, greatly improved state and federal cooperation, and added resources. What else can the U.S. government do?

First, we can widen and deepen legal immigration channels of various forms to provide greater legal access. Without it, we will always find ourselves in untenable positions both in regard to control efforts and public perceptions of the skill and ability to enforce policy. Second, we can systematically and regularly review internal controls with an eye to reducing opportunities for illegal aliens to gain footholds. One focus here must be on the labor market with intrinsic safeguards for the rights of the workers and to avoid the abuses of the Bracero era.[88] A third focus must be on all of the "law and order" issues and a more progressive interior enforcement strategy, with greater focus on preventing acts of terrorism, drug and people trafficking and removing criminal aliens from prisons and less focus on the apprehension of low-level visa abusers. Fourth, our government must entice the illegal aliens to come out of the shadows and abandon the unhealthy undergrounds they have created and provide a path to earn their way to legal status. In addition to the gains in labor market and social policy order, the security imperatives of identification are paramount. Fifth, our border control stance must be reviewed frequently with an eye to continuing only investments that make sense and deliver results. We must develop agreements between the countries with the greatest influx of illegal aliens (such as Mexico and Latin America) and focus on sharing responsibility for the management of migration flows. These agreements must be truly bilateral in nature and balanced in terms of what each country gives and gets in return.[89]

In the end, effective control and management of the laws against illegal immigration requires vigilant oversight and adequate resources. Those costs will be more than offset by savings to states, counties, communities, and school districts across the nation.

## Conclusion

Immigration is an intrinsic element of national security but the preponderance of immigration issues and concerns are not.[90] Illegal immigration into the U.S., perhaps more than any other issue, implies a degree of failure of countries to govern and provide for their people across the board in the policy sphere, from employment and living conditions to education to civil liberties.[91] In an odd manner, the tragic events of 11 September 2001 served as a reminder that the U.S., as a nation of immigrants, has grown more and more diverse since the 1965 amendments to the country's immigration laws. It also pointed out that this may be the country's very undoing.

While the U.S. has sought to regulate immigration to and from our country, the growing volume of illegal aliens demonstrates the inadequacy of national policy and immigration program management. It is clear the U.S. has not yet devised adequate strategies for coping with the continuing stream of illegal immigration. Already having an abundance of unskilled and poorly education adults, the last thing the U.S. needs is to continue to allow more such persons to immigrate illegally into the country. What is called for is a reversal of the benign neglect approach and a concerted and coordinated approach.[92] If not, at the current rate, by the year 2050, more than 42 million illegal aliens will be living in the U.S, crowding our cities and costing the government billions of dollars to support them. However complex the issue of illegal immigration is, the American people have a right to expect far greater accountability from the immigration system than they now get.

## Endnotes

[1] David W. Haines and Karen E. Rosenblum, *Illegal Immigration in America: A Reference Handbook* (Westport, C.T.: Greenwood Press, 1999), 1.

[2] Russell Pearce, "The Hard Truth on Illegal Immigration," available from http://www.alpinesurvival.com/russell-pearce_illegal-mexican-immigration.html; Internet; accessed 11 December 2006.

[3] Demetrios G. Papademetriou, "The Global Struggle with Illegal Migration: No End in Sight," *Migration Information Source*, 1 September 2005 [journal on-line]; available from http: www.migrationinformation.org/Feature/display.cfm?ID=336; Internet; accessed 12 December 2006.

18

[4] Jennifer Van Hook, "Unauthorized Migrants Living in the U.S.: A Mid-Decade Portrait," 1 September 2005, linked from the *Migration Policy Institute Home Page* at "Feature Story," available from http://www.migrationinformation.org/USfocus/display.cfm?ID=329; Internet; accessed 12 December 2006.

[5] Jeffrey S. Passel, "Unauthorized Migrants: Numbers and Characteristics," Background Briefing Prepared for the Task Force on Immigration and America's Future, 14 June 2005; available from http://pewhispanic.org/files/reports/46.pdf; Internet; accessed 12 November 2006, 3.

[6] Wikipedia, "Illegal Immigration", available from http://en.wipikedia.ord/wiki/illegal_migration; Internet; accessed 12 November 2006.

[7] George Weissinger, Ph.D., "The Illegal Alien Problem: Enforcing the Immigration Laws," 7 November 2003; available from http://www.immigration-usa.com/george_weissinger.html; Internet; accessed 12 November 2006.

[8] Haines, 1.

[9] Bill Ong Hing, *Defining American Through Immigration Policy* (Philadelphia: Temple University Press, 2004), ix.

[10] Robert W. Tucker, Charles B. Keely, and Linda Wrigley, *Immigration and U.S. Foreign Policy* (Boulder, CO.: Westview Press, 1990) 3.

[11] Samuel P. Huntington, "The Hispanic Challenge," *Foreign Policy Online*, March/April 2004 [journal on-line]; available from http://www.foreignpolicy.com/story/cms.php?story_id=2524; Internet; accessed on 12 November 2006, 31.

[12] Hing, 4.

[13] Huntington, 31.

[14] Ibid.

[15] Weissinger, 3.

[16] Huntington, 35.

[17] Wikipedia, "The Immigration Act of 1990," available from http://en.wikipedia.org/wiki/Immigration_Act_of_1990; Internet; accessed 12 November 2006.

[18] Weissinger, 3.

[19] Steven A. Carmarato, "Immigrants at Mid-Decade: A Snapshot of America's Foreign-Born Population in 2005," *The Center for Immigration Studies Backgrounder*, December 2005 [journal on-line]; available from http://www.cis.org/articles/2005/back1405.html; Internet; accessed 12 November 2006.

[20] Michael John Garcia and Ruth Ellen Wasem, *Immigration: Terrorist Grounds for Exclusion and Removal of Aliens* (Washington, D.C.: Congressional Research Service, 5 September 2006), 2.

[21] Hing, 132.

[22] Ibid.

[23] Haines, 113.

[24] Ibid, 135.

[25] Ibid, 123.

[26] Jeffrey S. Passel, *Estimates of the Size & Characteristics of the Undocumented Population* (Washington, D.C.: Pew Hispanic Center, 2005), 1.  Also, http://pewhispanic.org/reports/report/php?ReportID=44.

[27] Huntington, 34.

[28] Weissinger, 4.

[29] Haines, 25.

[30] Kenneth F. Johnson and Miles W. Williams, *Illegal Aliens in the Western Hemisphere: Political and Economic Factors* (New York: Praeger Publishing, 1981), 2.

[31] Ibid, 8.

[32] Ibid, 71.

[33] Haines, 232-250.

[34] Wikipedia, "Mexico", available from http://wikipedia.org/wiki/ Mexico#Economy; Internet; accessed on 2 December 2006.

[35] Haines, 3.

[36] Marti Dinerstein, "Social Security 'Totalization' Examining a Lopsided Agreement with Mexico," *Center for Immigration Studies Backgrounder,* September 2004 [journal on-line]; available from http://www.cis.org/articles/2004/back904.pdf; Internet; accessed 12 November 2006.

[37] The Center for Immigration Studies, "Illegal Immigration", available from http://www.cis.org/topics/illegalimmigration.html; Internet; accessed 12 November 2006.

[38] Passel, *Unauthorized Migrants: Numbers and Characteristics*, 4.

[39] Vernon M. Briggs, Jr., *Mass Immigration and the National Interest: Policy Directions for the New Century* (Armonk, NY: M.E. Sharpe, Inc., 2003), 4.

[40] Passel, *Unauthorized Migrants: Numbers and Characteristics*, 11-35.

[41] The Editors, "Border Security, Terrorism, and You," *Family Security Matters Online*, 4 December 2006 [journal on-line]; available from http://www.familysecuritymatters.org/homeland. Php?id-460575; Internet; accessed on 9 December 2006.

[42] Ibid.

[43] Janice L. Kephart, "Immigration and Terrorism: Moving Beyond the 9/11 Staff," panel discussion, National Press Club, Washington, D.C., 30 August 2005; available from http://www.cis.org/articles/2005/edwards-kephart-transcript.html#JANICE; Internet; accessed 9 December 2006.

[44] Jessica M. Vaughan, *America's New Welcome Mat: A Look at the Goals and Challenges of the US-VISIT Program Testimony before the U.S. House of Representatives Committee on Government Reform,* 4 March 2004; available from http:///www.cis.org/articles/2004/jessicatestimony030404.html; Internet; accessed 9 December 2006.

[45] Kephart, 18-19.

[46] Ibid, 28.

[47] Ely Karmon, "Hezbollah America Latina – Queer Group or Real Threat?" 7 November 2006, linked from The Institute for Counter-Terrorism Home Page at "*Spotlights*," available from http://www.ict.org.il/2006); Internet; accessed 10 November 2006, 1.

[48] The United States Department of State, "*Treasury Takes Aim at Hezbollah Fundraisers in Latin America,*" available from http://usinfo.state.gov/xarchives/display.html?p=washfile-english&y=2006&m=December&x=20061206141817esnamfuak0.1768762; Internet; accessed 4 January 2007.

[49] Karmon, 8.

[50] Karmon, 10.

[51] Angie C. Maerk, "Border Wars," *U.S. News and World Report Online*, 28 November 2005 [journal on-line]; available from http://www.usnews.com/usnews/news/articles/051128/28border.htm; Internet; accessed 7 January 2007, 1.

[52] Ibid, 2.

[53] Elliot Spagat, "Migrant Smugglers Benefit From Tougher Border Crossing," *Daily Bulletin Online*, 1 January 2007 [journal on-line]; available from http://www.dailybulletin.com/beyondborders/ci_4930503; Internet; accessed 7 January 2007.

[54] David Kyle and Rey Koslowski, *Global Human Smuggling* (Baltimore: John Hopkins University Press, 2001) 108-110.

[55] Kyle, 261.

[56] *The Human Trafficking Home Page*, available from http://www.humantrafficking.org/combat_trafficking/prevention; Internet; accessed 9 December 2006.

[57] Kyle, 344 - 345.

[58] *The United States Drug Enforcement Agency Home Page*, available from http://www.dea.gov/pubs/state_factsheets.html; Internet; accessed 7 January 2007.

[59] Wikipedia, "*Illegal Immigration*", available from http://en.wikipedia.ord/wiki/illegal_migration; Internet; accessed 12 November 2006.

[60] Heather McDonald, "The Immigrant Gang Plague," *City Journal Online,* Summer 2004 [journal on-line]; available from http://www.city-journal.org/html/14_3_immigrant_gang.html; Internet; accessed 6 January 2007.

[61] Joseph Farah, "Illegal Aliens Murder 12 Americans Daily: Death Toll in 2006 Far Overshadows Total U.S. Soldiers Killed in Iraq and Afghanistan," *WorldNet Daily Online*, 28 November 2006 [journal on-line]; available from http://www.worldnetdaily.com/news/article.asp?ARTICLE_ID=53103; Internet; accessed 7 January 2007.

[62] Ibid.

[63] "Study: One Million Sex Crimes by Illegals," *WorldNet Daily Online*, 31 May 2006 [journal on-line]; available from http://www.worldnetdaily.com/news/article.asp?ARTICLE_ID=50441; Internet; accessed 7 January 2007.

[64] Ibid.

[65] Farah.

[66] Ibid.

[67] Weissinger, 6.

[68] Haines, 14.

[69] Wikipedia, "Illegal Immigrant", available from http://en.wikipedia.org/wiki/illegal_immigrant#_note-7; Internet; accessed 12 November 2006.

[70] Ibid.

[71] Haines, 14-16.

[72] Ibid, 5.

[73] Ibid, 6.

[74] Erin Aubry Kaplan, "Piercing Black Silence on Immigration," Los Angeles Time, 17 January 2007; [newspaper on-line]; available from http://www.latimes.come/news/printededition/asection/la-oe-kaplan17jan17,1,5778992.column; Internet; accessed 20 January 2007.

[75] Wikipedia, "Illegal Immigrant"; available from http://en.wikipedia.org/wiki/Illegal_immigration#_note-7; accessed 12 November 2006.

[76] Haines, 7.

[77] Center for Immigration Studies, "The Cost of Illegal Immigration – Illegals Cost Feds $10 Billon a Year; Amnesty Would Nearly Triple Cost;" available from http://www/cis.org/articles/2004/fiscalrelease.html; Internet; accessed 9 January 2007.

[78] Ibid.

[79] Briggs, 280.

[80] Center for Immigration Studies, "Costs"; available from http://www.cis.org/topics/costs.html; Internet; accessed 26 September 2006.

[81] Dudley L. Poston, Jr., S Steven A. Camarota, and Amanda K. Baumle, "Remaking the Political Landscape: The Impact of Illegal and Legal Immigration on Congressional Apportionment," *The Center for Immigration Studies Backgrounder*, October 2003 [journal on-line]; available from http://www.cis.org/articles/2003/back1403.pdf; Internet; accessed 12 November 2006, 1-2.

[82] Ibid, 2.

[83] Huntington, 32.

[84] Ibid, 30.

[85] Ibid.

[86] Federation of American Immigration Reform (FAIR): "President's State of the Union Remarks on Immigration Will Highlight Why He is Not Trusted by the American Public," http://www.prenewswire.com/cgi-bin/stories.pl?ACCT= 104&STORY=/WWW.STORY/01-19-2; Internet; accessed 20 January 2007.

[87] Demetrios G. Papademetriou, "The Global Struggle with Illegal Migration: No End in Sight*," Migration Information Source*, 1 September 2005 [journal on-line]; available from http: www.migrationinformation.org/Feature/display.cfm?ID=336; Internet; accessed 12 December 2006, 4.

[88] Johnson, 71.

[89] Papademetriou, 6-7.

[90] Briggs, 274.

[91] Johnson, 181-185.

[92] Ibid.